How to Train Your *Cactus*

First published in Great Britain, Australia and New Zealand
in 2018 by Modern Books
An imprint of Elwin Street Productions Limited
14 Clerkenwell Green
London EC1R 0DP
www.modern-books.com

Illustrations by Tonwen Jones
Edited and with additional text by Elysse Bell and Jess Payn

ISBN: 978-1-911130-63-5

10 9 8 7 6 5 4 3 2 1

Printed in China

How to Train Your Cactus

A guide to raising
well-behaved succulents

TONWEN JONES

(m)

KEY

succulent

cactus

CONTENTS

HOW TO START
A PLANT FAMILY

INTRODUCTION

Cute, stylish, and low maintenance – what more could you want from a pet? For those of us who are not blessed with green fingers and have killed every plant we've ever touched, cacti and succulents are the perfect houseplants. They are easy-going roommates who will happily take up residence in your home and lend personality and pizzazz to interior spaces.

My own love of cacti was sparked early on, in the Kew Gardens conservatory in London. I was 7 or 8 years old at the time, and my grandmother had taken me to visit the plants. I was in awe of all the shapes, colours and crazy textures. Years later, I designed a map of India for display inside the conservatory – funny how things come full circle!

Cacti and succulents have continued to excite me over the years, featuring in my holiday plans (visiting the Majorelle Garden in Marrakech, Morocco), wedding decor (I had succulents in my bouquet and cacti as decorations!), home, and studio. I hope you too experience the joy of locking eyes with the perfect cactus and bringing it home with you, or making these funky green guys part of your interior decorating.

CHOOSE YOUR PLANT

Firstly, do you want a cactus or a succulent? This question is actually a bit misleading, as *all* cacti are succulents, and succulents are simply plants that store water; as a result, their leaves and stems are plump and adorable.

Cacti are a variety of succulent, differentiated by areoles: small, cushion-like, bumpy structures out of which hairs, spines, flowers and branches can (but may not) grow. Other succulent plants do not have areoles; however, to make matters confusing, not all cacti are prickly – that is, they have areoles but no spines – and some succulents have thorns, but these don't grow from areoles.

Basically, all cacti are succulents, but not all succulents are cacti. Succulents are diverse and encompass everything from rose-like clusters and spiky shoots to geometric candelabras and button-leaved sprouts. They hail mainly from savannahs and deserts (the ones in this book are largely from Africa, Australia and the Americas), but there are rainforest and jungle species too. As such, they love dry, warm climates and can go for a while without water, relying on their own storage system, making them a lovely, low-maintenance addition to any home!

READY YOUR HOME

So, you've decided to invite a characterful cactus or sociable succulent into your home! How do you ready your space?

First, choose a spot and make some room. They will be happiest with good access to sunlight, so rule out spaces without windows or decent sun. Make sure there's nothing in the way of your light source; let your new pals take centre stage under sunny spotlights. Check how much moisture your plant can take – some succulents are picky about humid environments, meaning the kitchen or bathroom won't be a good choice. A windowsill can be a pleasing perch, but hanging baskets, bookshelves, coffee tables, or plant stands work, too. Corners and heights are often underutilized spots and can create striking features.

Then, consider your container. Most succulents are happiest in pots slightly larger than they are; they won't grow well as lone islands in a sea of potting soil. Wider vessels drain better; the more and the deeper the soil in the pot, the more moisture is retained, which can cause problems. You can also house your plant pets in terrariums (see page 14). While most plants won't sprout wildly in your house, they usually appreciate a new pot (and maybe a new spot) each year or so, depending on growth.

FAMILY PLANNING

PROPAGATION

Plants' growth behaviours determine which method of reproduction is right for them. If they grow branches, columns, stems, or even just leaves, you can cut off side shoots, stems, and outer leaves with shears. These cuttings need to dry out and produce a callous on the site of the wound (ouch!) which might take a day to upwards of a week. During this time, leave them on a tray or plate until the raw end has healed over. Then, place your cuttings on top of a shallow tray filled with cactus or succulent soil – you can even arrange them in a pretty pattern for display, if you're doing lots. A few weeks later, you'll notice roots and miniature plantlets growing from the base of your cuttings. Until the roots appear, it's important not to overwater them, as they can easily rot – after they root, weekly should do it. Over time, the original plant stem or leaf will wither and you can carefully remove it. Replant your new baby once it's rooted in the tray of soil, being careful about direct sun exposure until it's more grown up.

Genuses that cluster, like *aloe*, *jovibarba*, and some cacti, will grow their own 'pups' right at their bases. Once these babies are 2 to 3 weeks old, check how much the roots have developed. If they're fairly rooted, remove them by cutting or even with a gentle twist, being careful to keep the existing roots intact. Then, follow the above steps!

GROWING FROM SEEDS

In spring, sow seeds in well-draining soil with added grit or sand. Little seeds should be distributed evenly, and not covered over by the soil; bigger ones should be snuggled in by one or two times the depth of their size. Gently mist the surface, then cover the pot with a glass cloche or plastic bag. It's best to keep this plant nursery at about 21°C, in partial shade so as not to disturb their sleep. Every day, air it out by removing the cover and wiping off condensation (or changing the bag) so that it's kept moist but not overly wet. Once seedlings develop a few weeks later, uncover and water only when the soil becomes dry. Spray the surface every so often to keep it moist. You can repot them about a year later, when they are large enough to handle. Using a fork or a spoon, gently wiggle them out and place them on top of a small, partially filled pot. Fill the remaining space with soil and give them a good drink!

THE MORE THE MERRIER!

What size of plant family is best for you? However many you have room and want to care for! You might be happy with a big family of foliage, but if you get overwhelmed, many people would love to be gifted a baby plant. Or, start your own business and spread the plant love even more!

WHAT YOU'LL NEED

SOIL
A well-draining cactus and/or succulent potting mix will usually do the trick. Have some on hand for repotting.

GRAVEL OR SMALL STONES
A layer at the bottom of your pot will help keep your succulents well-drained and happy.

CONTAINERS
As your plant collection grows, so will your assortment of containers. Clay and concrete are porous materials and, therefore, ideal for succulents, but plastic works too. Drainage holes are a must; if there isn't one in a pot you really like, don't sweat it! Either drill a hole, or keep your plant in its plastic pot inside your container to use it as a decorative case.

Or, if you're after something really special, craft your own, miniature green universe in a terrarium. Choose one that's 'open', so your plants have room to breathe, mind that the glass tends to magnify direct sun, and that these glass houses have no drainage holes (a gravel layer and frugal watering schedule are musts). Experiment with an array of plants, glass shapes, sizes and figurines.

WATERING VESSELS

Pick out a fun watering can to make your regular routine seem like less of a chore! A spray bottle also comes in handy for misting baby plant seeds.

NICE TO HAVES

- Trowels, for repotting (spoons work too).
- Heavy-duty gardening gloves for handling your prickly friends.
- A pair of tweezers or a cactus gripping tool for when you need to repot, prune, or propagate your buddy.
- A comb, for grooming those woolly types (see pages 104 and 120).
- A small paintbrush, for dusting your friends.
- Bedtime stories, to read to your plants before they go dormant. We plant parents take our job very seriously!

STYLING

Here's some inspiration to really let your plants show off:

COLOUR: Match plant and pot for a minimalist monochrome look, or set them off against each other for contrast. Think about the colours of paint or other elements in the room – do you want it to highlight or blend into the palette?

TEXTURE: Does your plant have a texture that the pot could enhance in some way? A spiky, ribbed cactus might look quite quirky placed in a spherical pot with ridges.

SHAPE: Smooth pots play up sculptural silhouettes, while geometric ones lend striking symmetry top to bottom.

NUMBERS: Odd numbers are visually pleasing (think threes and fives). Mix up textures, heights, and types – spiky, rounded, leafy, trailing, and tall. And remember that, while a crowd of plants can look lush and gorgeous, you'll have to water each separately. Pests and diseases spread readily among plants that are close together because of the dense foliage and higher humidity, so best allow for good air circulation and give them a bit of space to breathe.

TROUBLESHOOTING

Despite their famed hardiness as plant pets, cacti and succulents are not immortal and aren't immune to neglect or disease, needing a bit of tender loving care. Still, if you're mindful of the symptoms and advice below, it will be easy to nip problems in the bud, before there are any plant fatalities!

OVERWATERING

Overwatering is the number one cause of death among cacti and succulents. After all, most of them originally evolved in dry, desert-like conditions, so they adapted to store their own water and therefore won't need much assistance on that front. These hardy hooligans will quickly get upset if they think you're trying to drown them: watch out for yellow, wilting leaves; mushy or rotting roots, stems or leaves; or healthy leaves falling off at the slightest touch. If you've overdone it on the hydration, wait for the soil to dry out or repot your plant entirely, trimming off any rotten roots and patches beforehand.

Underwatering is much less of a problem, so when in doubt, wait it out! Cacti might shrink or turn purple or reddish when they're thirsty, while other succulents might signal thirst with wrinkly, dry-looking leaves, or by sagging and drooping. If they get to that point, they will perk up again after one or two drinks.

Humidity in general is also something to watch out for. Corky scabs might show up on your cacti if they're struggling in an overly humid habitat; moisture can also encourage the spread of pests and fungal disease, and worsen problems like root rot. Some plants like to be taken outside in the summer to help them dry or air out a bit.

ROOM TEMPERATURE

One of the reasons why succulents are such excellent companions is that they are fairly comfortable at room temperature, or in the range of temperatures of an average home. They like it a bit warmer in the summer, and a bit cooler in the winter, making a windowsill a lovely, comfortable plant habitat.

Extreme heat can cause some succulents to change colour – you'll notice a warm, golden glow. This can recede if moved to a cooler environment. Most succulents are fairly hardy, but won't tolerate cold all too well; some cacti can develop brown marks if they're chilly. In general, let your houseplants acclimatize slowly if the temperature has fluctuated to either extreme.

TOO MUCH SUNLIGHT

Succulents love sunshine, but there is absolutely such a thing as too much. Cacti can develop corky scabs in overly bright conditions; further spread can be prevented by very gradually reducing the light. Succulents can get sunburned – their leaves may scorch in too much direct sun, leaving permanent brown, white, or pale patches on the leaves; extreme cases can even cause dry, black or crispy leaves. In an ideal amount of sun, some succulents may react by changing their hues – botanical 'blush'!

If your pets aren't getting enough sun, some of them might turn pale or yellow, and/or reach towards the light source, stretching themselves out in the process (the fancy term for this is 'etiolation'). This isn't necessarily a problem – in fact, it can lead to some pretty funky-looking shapes – unless it gets to the point of weakening your plant's overall structure. They just don't know when to stop, poor things! If you notice your plant searching for the light, move it closer or give it some more.

For safety, keep delicate or dangerous plants where they won't be disturbed – or disturb you, pets, or kids. Some species are poisonous, skin irritants, or not very cuddly.

PESTS AND DISEASES

You adopted one pet . . . but it's brought a little entourage with it. Yuck! Here's how to recognize what these unwelcome guests look like and how to escort them out of your plant party.

GNATS: These tiny flies might gather around if soil stays too wet for too long; consider a better-draining mixture and let it dry out between each plant drink.

MEALYBUGS: These annoying insects might leave small balls of white fluffy wax, orange-pink eggs, or sticky 'honeydew' on your plant pet, the last of which encourages the growth of black mould. You can kill them with rubbing alcohol (70% isopropyl should do the trick), which you can dab on with a cotton swab or mist over with a spray bottle.

SCALE INSECTS: True to their name, these look like flat or slightly rounded brown scales and might show up if you've given your plant a field trip outdoors during the summer. An insecticidal spray will discourage them from returning.

RED SPIDERS: Almost microscopically small; you're more likely to notice brown dots, scarring or webbing on your plant. Red spiders dislike humidity, so try misting your plant to get rid of them.

VINE WEEVILS: A large, black beetle-looking guy with long antennae that will lay eggs in your soil that hatch into white, brown-headed larvae (how rude!). Babies and adults love to nibble roots, stems and leaves, so if you notice some bites in your plants you might have one of these visitors. If you see any larvae in your potting mix, repot your plant.

FUNGAL ROT: A variety of types exist with different symptoms, but if you notice brown, grey or black spots, fungus, stem rot or rotting black tissue, you'll want to cut off the infected bits and treat them with fungicide. Quarantining your plant by moving it to a different area, away from its friends, is a good way to prevent spread.

50 CACTI AND
SUCCULENTS
and how to train them

Aeonium arboreum var. atropurpureum

TREE HOUSELEEK

Looking for an easygoing and easy-growing companion? Look no further than this purple playmate. A plum-coloured rosette composed of shiny fleshy leaves perches on a branching stem, resembling an overgrown flower or mini tree.

Training notes

MAXIMUM SIZE: Leaves up to 8 cm (3 in) long; branches up to 1 m (3 ft) high and 1.2 m (4 ft) wide after a prosperous 5 to 10 years.

SOIL: Rests easy in a sandy, loam-based mix; gets hungry monthly in growing season for half-strength balanced liquid fertilizer.

WATER: From winter to spring, whenever soil feels dry; let the top 1 cm (½ in) of soil dry out between waterings. In summer, only thirsty when leaves start to curl.

FLOWERS: Small, star-shaped; mature plants flower in winter, but at a cost – rosettes die after flowering.

WATCH OUT FOR: Root rot; overly long stems might snap if rosettes are heavy, but can be used for new plant babies!

Styling notes

Houseleeks adore full sunlight and enjoy the respite of afternoon or partial shade in summer. A bit of moisture keeps them perky, so a bathroom windowsill makes a good home.

COPPER PINWHEEL

This exuberant white-green beauty hails from the Canary Islands and is named for her shape and copper-edged blooms. If you're lucky enough to track her down in a shop, she's a stylish addition to any family of flora, but watch out – she'll make other plants jealous.

Training notes

MAXIMUM SIZE: Up to 45 cm (18 in) tall and 20 cm (8 in) across.

SOIL: Likes a sandy, dry-to-medium moist mix.

WATER: Regularly in summer growing season; in winter, only if soil completely dries out.

FLOWERS: White-yellow; only mature plants make this fatal trade-off – plants die after flowering.

WATCH OUT FOR: Root rot – chop off the rotten end and place the leaf in soil to bring it to life as a new plant.

Styling notes

The sassy sunburst is defined by sun thirst – full sunlight or bright shade is a must. Park your pinwheel in a sunny, airy room that isn't too humid; she'll happily play the role of jaunty bookshelf accessory or stunning coffee table feature if given appropriate stage lighting.

KIWI AEONIUM

With brilliantly hued, chubby, spoon-shaped leaves that grow in a circular rosette, the kaleidoscopic Kiwi is an extremely colourful character: one of my very favourite succulents for this reason. Also known as a 'Tricolour' Aeonium, it develops its vibrant colours by soaking up sun.

Training notes

MAXIMUM SIZE: 60 cm to 1 m (2 to 3 ft) tall and wide.

SOIL: Happiest in semi-moist sandy loam or regular potting mix; eats half-strength fertilizer monthly in winter.

WATER: Regularly in winter growing season, but only when the top few centimetres/inch of soil are thoroughly dry. Will coyly curl its leaves when thirsty.

FLOWERS: Yellow; mature plants may decide to show them off in summer as a decorative denouement before they die.

WATCH OUT FOR: Root rot; scorching.

Styling notes

Keep your Kiwi in a spot with partial sun; it craves just enough light to develop its gorgeous hues, but doesn't like too much heat and can burn if it goes overboard on the sunbathing. As it makes a striking accent piece in any bright room I keep mine in an open terrarium to really let it show off.

Agave americana

CENTURY PLANT

Named for the (incorrect) assumption that this slender, spiny grey-green ruffian flowers once a century (though it may only live to 20). Also answers to 'American Aloe' on account of its southern US and Mexican origins.

Training notes

MAXIMUM SIZE: Wild: up to 1.8 m (6 ft) tall and 3 m (10ft) wide!

SOIL: Digs standard, well-draining cactus mix with grit and gravel; approves of balanced liquid fertilizer every couple of weeks in summer.

WATER: Regularly in summer; only when soil dries out completely in winter.

FLOWERS: A rare, dramatic and fatal gesture from mature plants (ten years or older); after sending up tree-like yellow shoots, agave will bid the world adieu.

WATCH OUT FOR: Scale insects; moisture – excess humidity may cause leaves to turn white and blotchy.

Styling notes

This dashing desert specimen gets a kick out of full, direct sunlight. Makes a striking centrepiece among several small succulents. As it grows and needs repotting, play with pot styles to match or offset its subtle tint and texture.

ALOE VERA

This spiky fellow is known for its healing properties –
ancient Greeks believed it could even cure baldness and
insomnia. It's also easy to grow and, with its angular,
grey-green, gem-like leaves, easy on the eyes . . . Say 'Aloe'
to your new best friend!

Training notes

MAXIMUM SIZE: Can grow 60 cm to 1 m (2 to 3 ft) tall and wide
(after 5 to 10 years).

SOIL: Likes a sandy and well-draining mixture.

WATER: More frequently in summer growing season; drench
soil but let it dry out completely in between drinks. Thin
curled leaves mean Aloe is thirsty.

FLOWERS: These are rare. Greenish-yellow; in summer.

WATCH OUT FOR: Mealybugs; pet interaction – it's poisonous!

Styling notes

Aloe likes natural light, though avoid direct sunlight. As
happy on a windowsill as perched on a bookshelf, a wide,
well-draining pot is a must wherever Aloe hangs out. On
reaching maturity, Aloe might grow more leaves and
shoots, which you can propagate to grow your plant
family. Prune any pinkish-brown tips or leaves, or harvest
up to one-third of the green leaves at a time for their gel.

FISHHOOK CACTUS

I'm hooked on this adorably round, spiky cactus, with its distinguished crisscrossing fishhook-shaped spines. Looking for a slow-growing and extremely easygoing companion? This is my pick.

Training notes

MAXIMUM SIZE: 15 cm (6 in) tall, 10 cm (4 in) in diameter; may grow in clusters of three or four.

SOIL: Takes well to very dry, gritty/sandy cactus soil.

WATER: Doesn't care much for it. Not thirsty at all in the winter, and will only drink in spring and summer when its soil is completely dry.

FLOWERS: You may be able to coax it to sprout a delicate pink flower from the crown of its head in early spring.

WATCH OUT FOR: Root rot – do not overwater!

Styling notes

Choose a deep pot to accommodate its large root system, and let it live in a sunny, airy room – Fishhooks appreciate direct sunlight with as little humidity as possible. I like to show off mine's stout stature by placing it next to a tall-fronded friend like an aloe, haworthia or sanseveria for a study in contrasts.

Astrophytum myriostigma

BISHOP'S HAT

Bishop's Hat is a bit of a cowardly (read: spineless) comrade, making it a great pick if you don't want to be pricked. A stout, star-shaped fellow with leaves that resemble a paper fortune-teller, this is one of the only cacti you can comfortably pet!

Training notes

MAXIMUM SIZE: 20 cm (8 in) tall, 20 to 30 cm (8 to 12 in) wide, but this may take 20 years.

SOIL: Fond of porous cactus soil, containing some loam or peat if possible. Feed during growing season with a balanced, diluted fertilizer such as a 20-20-20 mix.

WATER: Not very thirsty; drinks sporadically in summer and not at all during wintertime..

FLOWERS: In summer, might reveal large, light yellow flowers, followed by red or green berries.

WATCH OUT FOR: Overwatering; aphids, scale insects and mealybugs. Yuck!

Styling notes

Leave your Hat in the sun for hours a day in summer, though give it a bit of a break from the heat in the winter months. Papery-looking leaves and angular folds make the Bishop's Hat a funky geometric desk accessory.

Austrocylindropuntia subulata

EVE'S PIN

A green, cylindrical, bristly gal, Eve's leaves are stubby and barrel shaped. Though comically oversized when small, they grow in the company of fierce, sharp needles when she's matured to a riper age – so watch out for her bite!

Training notes

MAXIMUM SIZE: Can grow up to 4 m (13 ft) tall in the wild, and, for this reason, often acts as a natural fence in her high-altitude home in the Andes of Ecuador and Peru.

SOIL: Comfortable in standard, well-draining cactus soil.

WATER: Weekly in summer, letting the soil dry out between drinks. Only thirsty in winter if she shrivels her leaves.

FLOWERS: May show off her bright red flowers, followed by red fruits, in the summer.

WATCH OUT FOR: Rapid growth!

Styling notes

Eve fancies partial shade to full sun, so she'll enjoy relaxing in a bright bedroom or window that gets a moderate amount of light. If she likes you, she may grow extremely tall, so pick a pot and a spot that can accommodate her ambition, and repot whenever she outgrows her current trappings.

NIGHTFLOWERING CACTUS

Distinguished by upright, climbing columns, with spines that protrude in vertical lines along distinct ribs, this characterful creature is named for its wild behaviour: in its native Florida, it will blossom, but only once, at night.

Training notes

MAXIMUM SIZE: 1.8 to 2.4 m (4 to 8 ft) tall; width depends on sprawl.

SOIL: Well-draining. Provide monthly feasts of cactus fertilizer (any brand will do) in summer.

WATER: Soak the soil weekly in summer and let it dry out completely before watering again. Slumbers through the winter, so a drink once every few weeks is enough.

FLOWERS: A dramatic and mysterious affair, if you're lucky enough to experience it. Fragrant, trumpet-shaped white flowers open as night falls, and wilt by dawn.

WATCH OUT FOR: Scorching.

Styling notes

An airy room with plenty of sun and heat is a 'cereus'-ly great choice; let it welcome guests to your home by setting it in the foyer. A clay or terracotta pot is an elegant outfit.

MING THING

This Argentinian amigo is one that only a (plant) parent could love: an alien-looking variant of *Cereus forbesii*, its quirky growth pattern is driven by a genetic mutation that convinces each tip it's the dominant one, making it compete with the others.

Training notes

MAXIMUM SIZE: Up to 30 cm (12 in) tall and 45 cm (18 in) across; most houseplants are roughly 9 cm (3½ in) tall and wide.

SOIL: Likes to hunker down in gravelly, well-draining soil.

WATER: Needs a weekly drink in summer; make sure the soil is dry before watering again. Not at all thirsty in winter and, in fact, is liable to swell up if given too much!

FLOWERS: None. Boo-hoo.

WATCH OUT FOR: Root rot; humidity; rapid growth (repot this guy as often as necessary).

Styling notes

Plenty of filtered sun suits this strange creature best. Try a windowsill perch that gets light for part of the day, and avoid humidity at all costs – no bathroom or kitchen.

Ceropegia woodii

STRING OF HEARTS

This girl tugs at the heartstrings. Romantic trailing stems, dotted with marbled silver leaves, flow gracefully about. When vines get too long, use the prunings to produce more gorgeous plant babies. Simply cut off four or five sections of stem, 10 to 15 cm (4 to 6 in) long, leaving at least one leaf on each, and plant them in a pot of sterilized soil; cover with a cloche to keep them warm and moist.

Training notes

MAXIMUM SIZE: 1 m (3 ft) spread after about 2 to 5 years.
SOIL: Loves a well-draining sandy, loamy cactus mix and a low-nitrogen liquid fertilizer two or three times a year.
WATER: Not very thirsty; only when soil is completely dry.
FLOWERS: Will accessorize in summer with pink or purple lantern-shaped drops, sometimes followed by cylindrical fruits with silky, tufted seeds.
WATCH OUT FOR: Basal rot in winter; cold temperatures. Leaves will turn yellow if she's cold or overwatered!

Styling notes

String of hearts is your ideal candidate for hanging baskets and tall shelves. She's a dainty and affable dame that enjoys the sun but is fairly forgiving, so she'll be comfortable in most rooms.

Coryphantha sulcata

PINEAPPLE CACTUS

Guess where this guy gets its name? Look no further than its curious flowering habits – when in bloom, this plump, tubercled chum resembles a perky pineapple. But watch out for those star-shaped spikes!

Training notes

MAXIMUM SIZE: 8 to 12 cm (3 to 5 in) wide and tall.

SOIL: Will be grateful for sandy, gritty cactus mix with some quartz gravel and pumice. Feed once per summer with cacti fertilizer diluted to half strength.

WATER: Turns its nose up at too much water, so water minimally in summer and keep fairly dry in winter.

FLOWERS: On top of its big round head! May show off white/pink flowers in early spring or gold flowers in late spring.

WATCH OUT FOR: Too much humidity – prone to rot; red spiders; mealybugs.

Styling notes

Like its tropical fruit counterpart, this Pineapple grows best in full sun, though it favours drier conditions, so make sure it's at home in an airy room with great ventilation. Choose a fairly shallow pot to accommodate the fibrous roots and to ensure good drainage – your bulbous buddy will be unbearably cute perched on a wide, low throne.

Crassula arborescens

SILVER DOLLAR PLANT

With round, stately grey-green leaves edged in signature maroon, the Silver Dollar is a wonderfully calming plant to 'spend' time with. Look closely and you might notice a speckling of reddish spots on the surface of the leaves.

Training notes

MAXIMUM SIZE: As an outdoor shrub, up to 1.2 m (4ft) tall and 1.8 to 2.7 m (6 to 9 ft) across.

SOIL: Relishes well-draining, slightly acidic (pH 6.0) succulent mix; gets hungry at the start of summer for controlled-release fertilizer.

WATER: Moderate thirst in summer (only once two-thirds of the soil has dried out); in winter, indulge monthly.

FLOWERS: A rare wintertime phenomenon! Lucky you if you get to see its white/light pink flowers.

WATCH OUT FOR: Mealybugs; fungal disease; overwatering.

Styling notes

Silver dollar likes to bask in sunlight on a windowsill. Any room will do, though its subtle, round leaves are a great addition to any space that could use an elegant touch. Pair it with a textured pot for maximum impact.

BUDDHA'S TEMPLE

If you've ever wanted to own a Shar Pei but can't, fear not! Get a Buddha's Temple instead – with their towers of tightly stacked, folded leaves, they're all adorable creases and good behaviour – and much less maintenance.

Training notes

MAXIMUM SIZE: Up to 15 cm (6 in) tall.

SOIL: Will be pleased with well-draining, slightly acidic (pH 6.0) succulent mix; likes a start of summer snack of controlled-release fertilizer.

WATER: Not thirsty during summer dormancy; in winter growing season, allow soil to dry completely before giving your Buddha a drink.

FLOWERS: A collection of tiny red, orange, or white buds from the top of the plant; occurs at any point in the year!

WATCH OUT FOR: Mealybugs; fungal disease; overwatering.

Styling notes

This easy-going fellow will revel in any bright room, but likes to avoid direct sunlight in summertime. Place him anywhere needing a geometric accent – on a table or a windowsill in a tiled bathroom or kitchen. Choose a pot with a complementary texture or shape.

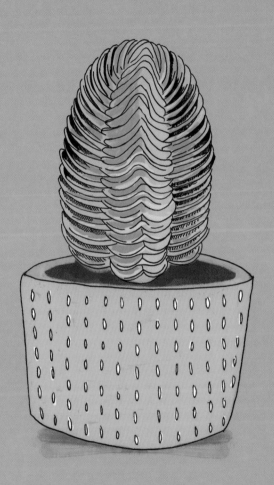

WATCH CHAIN

In her native Africa, this Medusa-like madam grows bushy and wild – a riot of gorgeous green! At home, she's more at ease and loves to lazily extend her curiously textured, slender branching stems into the air.

Training notes

MAXIMUM SIZE: 15 to 20 cm (6 to 8 in) tall.

SOIL: Will take kindly to a well-draining, slightly acidic (pH 6.0) succulent mix; craves controlled-release fertilizer at the beginning of summer.

WATER: In summer dormancy, not very thirsty; fancies regular drinks in winter growing season but only when soil is completely dry.

FLOWERS: Tiny yellow-green flowers in spring but (how indelicate!) release a rather pungent, acrid cat-urine smell.

WATCH OUT FOR: Overwatering; mealybugs; fungus.

Styling notes

Her vivacious verdant tendrils are perfect in a hanging basket anywhere warm, brightly lit, and with low humidity, like a dining room window.

Crassula ovata

MONEY PLANT

A popular good luck charm, the Money Plant also goes by the name 'Friendship Tree' – which is either a lovely nod towards sharing prosperity or a sour outlook on friendship and bribery! A thick-branched evergreen with shiny, smooth leaves, its sumptuous green colour makes it the perfect addition to a group of colourful succulents.

Training notes

MAXIMUM SIZE: 1 m (3 ft) tall.

SOIL: Happiest in gritty, well-draining mix. Enjoys balanced liquid feed – indulge every two to three weeks.

WATER: Moderately thirsty from spring to fall and abstains during the rest of the year.

FLOWERS: Can sprout cheerful clusters of starry white or light pink flowers in late summer.

WATCH OUT FOR: Root rot; mealybugs, aphids and vine weevils; interaction with other pets – it's poisonous!

Styling notes

Quite the sunbather, your Money Tree will like to lounge somewhere with a lot of light. Its luscious leaves can make it top-heavy, so choose a sturdy pot that will minimize its chances of toppling over.

HORN TREE

A diminutive shrub with glossy green tubular fingers, tipped in coppery-red, Horn Tree, alias Trumpet Jade, could also go by 'Pipe Organ Plant'. A symphony of smooth, its leaves aspire to heavenly heights – or, at least, however much it's able to achieve from an earthly pot.

Training notes

MAXIMUM SIZE: 80 cm (32 in) tall, 40 cm (16 in) wide.

SOIL: Well-draining sandy cactus compost is music to its ears; feed it three times a summer with 10-10-10 fertilizer.

WATER: Slight thirst in summer; allow soil to dry completely in between waterings. Not a big drinker in winter.

FLOWERS: Pinkish-white star-like blooms in winter – as if mimicking snowflakes!

WATCH OUT FOR: Mealybugs, aphids, and vine weevils will gather around it for a feast; ensure pets aren't liable to do the same as it is poisonous!

Styling notes

This graceful Crassula makes a good bonsai tree. Terracotta pots ensure good air movement through the soil and balance inevitable top-heaviness. It will shine in full sunlight but might let you get away with shadier situations – pick a bright, airy spot for best results.

Crassula pellucida

CALICO KITTEN

A low-growing, 'low'-key pet, this groundhugger likes to relax slowly outward, taking up ever-so-slightly more room than it needs. Heart-shaped yellow leaves feature a central green stripe and are edged in red: the calico of its name refers to this pleasing mix of hues. As precious as its namesake, though not quite as snuggly, Calico Kitten is a great alternative to pet ownership.

Training notes

MAXIMUM SIZE: Up to 15 cm (6 in) tall.

SOIL: Think rugged coastal beach getaway meets indoor planter: porous, well-draining soil with rocks or sand.

WATER: Fancies a weekly drink, or whenever it's feeling dry.

FLOWERS: Whitish star-shaped flowers appear in late spring or early summer.

WATCH OUT FOR: Mealybugs; fungal disease (gross).

Styling notes

Striking geometric strands love to hang from suspended baskets, though don't be afraid to give them a haircut when they get out of control. Direct sunlight makes Kitten blush red – so let it stay cool in filtered light, with some shade in the summertime.

Crassula perforata

STRING OF BUTTONS

Aptly named for her neat, beanstalk-like growth pattern,
this South African sprite grows as a shrub in the wild.
Light and bright is her signature: she sprouts green leaves
with reddish edges and a chalky white bloom on the
surface, and grows more colourful, yellow leaves with a
blue-green stripe and red edges at the top of each cluster.
A graceful ager, older leaves darken to a gentle blue-green.

Training notes

MAXIMUM SIZE: 60 cm (2 ft) tall to 1 m (3 ft) wide.
SOIL: Well-draining, slightly acidic (pH 6.0) soil; has a
hankering for a controlled-release fertilizer at the
beginning of the summer.
WATER: Once a week in summer; give her the odd shower
during winter dormancy but test the soil for complete
dryness in between waterings.
FLOWERS: Pale yellow in spring – a pleasant pastel party!
WATCH OUT FOR: Mealybugs; fungal diseases – treat any cuts
(ouch!) with a fungicide so she doesn't get an infection.

Styling notes

Pale green and red, Buttons is a nice colourful accent for
any room with a mix of sun and shade and is a lovely
choice for terrariums, given a suitable drainage situation.

60

Echeveria affinis

BLACK ECHEVERIA

Fleshy triangular leaves form small, compact rosettes; babies start out green but slowly darken to a deep blackish brown. This gregarious master plays nicely with others and has been spotted relaxing in many a rock garden and trendy pot.

Training notes

MAXIMUM SIZE: 12 cm (5 in) tall to 25 cm (10 in) wide.

SOIL: Appreciates a slightly acidic (pH 6.0), well-draining succulent mix and being treated to controlled-release fertilizer at the beginning of summer.

WATER: Takes a weekly drink in summer, but only when its soil has dried out; mostly refrains from winter drinking.

FLOWERS: Will stretch out long arching stems in late summer to early autumn and produce cream-coloured blossoms.

WATCH OUT FOR: Root rot; dead leaves (mealybugs congregate there); stretching; fungal disease.

Styling notes

Try making a mini rock garden. A shallow, wide pot with some friends makes for a great plant party; you can even add ornaments, miniature figures or architectural features if you feel wild. Echeveria needs a few hours per day of direct sunlight but watch for browning leaves in hotter months.

CURLY LOCKS

This curly cutie has frilly, pale green leaves that grow in a spiralling rosette. Rumoured to have healing properties (it's said that chewing her leaves relieves toothache, and sliced leaves soothe inflamed skin), she's a green goddess!

Training notes

MAXIMUM SIZE: Mature madams can reach up to 25 cm (10 in) in diameter and 30 cm (12 in) tall.

SOIL: Likes her soil with a slight bite: slightly acidic (pH 6.0), well-draining succulent mix suits her best; feed her controlled-release fertilizer at the beginning of summer.

WATER: Once a week in summer, underneath her leaves. If she luxuriates in water, she can discolour. Indulge her every 2 to 4 weeks in winter to prevent leaves shrivelling.

FLOWERS: A bold bright orange or red, in spring to summer.

WATCH OUT FOR: Dead leaves underneath act as a haven for mealybugs; root rot; fungal disease; stretching.

Styling notes

Arrange a playdate with other echeveria in a shallow, wide bowl for a mini succulent garden, varying colors and textures for maximum cuteness. Perch your plant playground on a sill that gets a mix of sun and shade.

Echeveria elegans

MEXICAN SNOWBALL

A bit of an ice queen, Mexican Snowball is a luminous, elusive and refined rosette. Her blue-grey to silvery green leaves are the hardiest of her Echeveria amigos and can cope with temperatures dipping to -4°C.

Training notes

MAXIMUM SIZE: 20 cm (8 in) tall and 30 cm (12 in) wide.

SOIL: Slightly acidic (pH 6.0) to match her attitude – well-draining succulent mix should work well. Demands controlled-release fertilizer at the beginning of summer.

WATER: Only when soil feels dry and not at all during her long winter nap. How would you like to have water poured on you when you're sleeping?

FLOWERS: Yellow flowers on hot-pink arching stems in late winter and spring. A real statement!

WATCH OUT FOR: Root rot; stretching; fungal disease; mealybugs making a home in dead leaves.

Styling notes

A true windowsill woman, Snowball needs decent sun. Let her show off her icy leaves by placing her alongside other plants with contrasting shapes and colours.

Echeveria 'Perle von Nürnberg'

PEARL OF NÜRNBERG

With pale, greyish-brown rosettes composed of tapering, dusty leaves, Pearl is in high demand for floral arrangements and wedding bouquets. She was even honoured with the Award of Garden Merit by the Royal Horticultural Society! Even though she keeps such distinguished company, she'll happily take up in your home any day of the week.

Training notes

MAXIMUM SIZE: 15 cm (6 in) wide.

SOIL: Pearl likes a slightly acidic (pH 6.0), well-draining succulent mix; she'll be happy with a dose of controlled-release fertilizer at the beginning of summer.

WATER: Regularly in spring and summer; monthly in winter.

FLOWERS: This floral high achiever might offer up pink and yellow blossoms on reddish stems up to five to six times a year.

WATCH OUT FOR: Root rot; fungal disease; dead leaves (which are a mealybug's gathering beacon); stretching.

Styling notes

Pearl's elegant colour and shape makes her a grand choice for a sunny windowsill in any room that will benefit from her stately presence – try a bathroom or nursery.

Echinocactus grusonii

GOLDEN BARREL CACTUS

Barry is a jovial fellow with a bit of a beer belly, and can live for up to 30 years. Young Barry is knobbly, but as he ages, he'll grow up to 35 distinct ribs and elongate upwards.

Training notes

MAXIMUM SIZE: 1 to 1.2 m (3 to 4 ft) tall after 10 to 20 years, and about half as wide – larger in the wild!

SOIL: Sandy and loamy is Barry's pick; add pebbles or gravel to the bottom few centimetres/inch of his pot for the best drainage. A monthly summer feast of balanced liquid fertilizer will make him smile.

WATER: Enforce a strict drinking moratorium in winter, but ease up in summer – he can drink if his soil goes dry.

FLOWERS: Barry may crown himself with small, bell-shaped yellow flowers in summer, but only after about 20 years.

WATCH OUT FOR: His spikes! Much to his dismay, mealybugs love him and he is prone to root rot. Make sure he gets enough sun or he'll be grouchy.

Styling notes

A native Mexican, Barry likes a warm room with lots of sun and some fresh air. Change his outfit yearly when he's young so he has room to grow his personal style.

Echinopsis aurea

GOLDEN EASTER LILY CACTUS

Particularly prickly, this lone grower keeps to herself. Named for her exuberant yellow flowers, which open around Easter time, Lily is an otherwise moody green, globular gal with 14 to 15 sharp-edged ribs separated by deep grooves.

Training notes

MAXIMUM SIZE: 15 cm (6 in) tall, 4 to 10 cm (1½ to 4 in) in diameter.
SOIL: Unfussy – standard cactus mix will do.
WATER: Regularly; don't let her pot go bone dry when she's budding. Cut down on drinking in the autumn.
FLOWERS: Blooms throughout the year sprout implausibly from all over and can even obscure Lily's body, though these last only for one day.
WATCH OUT FOR: Her spikes!

Styling notes

Lily's shallow root system is cosiest in a shorter pot. Put her somewhere inaccessible but visible where she can show off; highlight her gold blooms with complementary colours. She'll want maximum sun and heat in the spring for flowering, but partial shade is fine the rest of the year.

Echinopsis chamaecereus

PEANUT CACTUS

Peanut is a wild thing, waving his chubby, clumped arms in the air like he's at a music festival. Soft, white bristles form his daring 'do.

Training notes

MAXIMUM SIZE: Stems can reach 15 cm (6 in) tall and up to 1.5 cm (½ in) in diameter.

SOIL: Rich and fast draining – like a rock star's bank account.

WATER: A bit thirstier than most other succulents; give him water when his soil is nearly, but not completely, dry. An occasional mist suits him best during wintertime.

FLOWERS: Dramatic red-orange beauties in the spring, if you're fortunate enough to coax them out.

WATCH OUT FOR: Mealybugs; scale insects; spider mites (usually in the wintertime).

Styling notes

Have some fun with his textured topography – Peanut is all about the drama and will play along as long as he is in a well-draining pot. In the summer growing season he appreciates strong sunlight and would even enjoy a field trip outside, though take it easy while he acclimatizes to the sunlight so he doesn't burn.

Euphorbia acurensis

DESERT CANDLE

True to its name, though looks can be deceiving: this grand candelabra resembles a cactus but is actually a succulent. True cacti have spines arising from areoles (small, circular features) while this one has thorns. I love the small, delicate leaves that grow at the top of its stems, which it sheds yearly.

Training notes

MAXIMUM SIZE: 3 m (10 ft) tall; grows to width of container.

SOIL: Well-draining, with a mix of sand, chalk, and loam; fertilize with half-strength feed monthly.

WATER: A regular drinker; once a week in summer but let the soil dry out in between.

FLOWERS: Small yellow-green flowers in springtime.

WATCH OUT FOR: The white milky sap (latex) it oozes when cut – it's poisonous and can cause skin irritation. Desert Candle is also poisonous to cats and dogs.

Styling notes

Not many plants hold a candle to this desert native's greed for sun. But don't expose it too much to direct rays, or it risks getting burnt. Near a window is best, and weigh it down in a heavy pot as it grows.

76

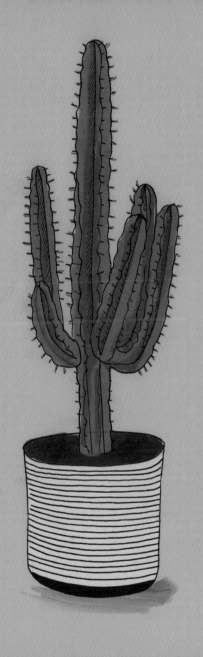

Euphorbia milii

CROWN OF THORNS

A grey-brown, spiky shrub with leaves that widen near the tip. So named as, when in bloom, it resembles Christ's crown with red droplets of blood. Many gain a sense of 'euphorbia' from owning this plant as it is easy to grow.

Training notes

SOIL: 1.8 m (6 ft) wide (after 10 to 20 years).
SOIL: Well-draining sand, chalk and loam; fertilize with half-strength feed monthly.
WATER: Oblige with a weekly soak; it doesn't tolerate drought well. Let the soil dry in between showers.
FLOWERS: A rare year-round bloomer; produces tiny red, pink, yellow, or white flowers flanked by a conspicuous pair of colourful bracts (a leaf or petal-like structure).
WATCH OUT FOR: The thorns! Also, all parts of this plant are poisonous – wear gloves when handling and avoid contact with skin, mouth or eyes.

Styling notes

Crown of Thorns will soak up the sun for part of the day and needs good air circulation and a well-draining pot. Allow it a wide berth so no one (pets, kids, and yourself included) touches it by mistake.

Euphorbia tirucalli

PENCIL CACTUS

A cactus by name, but a succulent in truth, this sketchy shrub resembles a pot full of unruly pencils. Its chameleon stems glow a fiery, festive red in wintry months (lending it the nickname: 'Sticks on Fire'), and mellow yellow in summer.

Training notes

MAXIMUM SIZE: A sprawling 7.5 m (25 ft) high and 3 m (10 ft) wide.

SOIL: Of slightly sour temperament, it's less grouchy in a slightly acidic home (pH 6.0 or so) with decent drainage. Temper with a controlled-release fertilizer at the beginning of the season.

WATER: A generous weekly drink in summer. Less in winter, but careful: though this squirt's thirstier than most, it's still prone to root rot.

FLOWERS: Pale, yellow, small: unlikely to enthral.

WATCH OUT FOR: The deadly milky sap. Broken stems leak a pretty pernicious residue that can poison you, irritate your skin, and burn your eyes, so wear gloves when handling.

Styling notes

Enliven your fiery friend by setting it on a bright sill: it likes full sunlight. Allowed to grow wild in its home habitats, it is sometimes used as a hedge, so it could be a nice accent in places where you want a bit of privacy.

FRED IVES GRAPTOVERIA

Meet the murky Fred Ives: a hybrid rosette and tricky to pin down. Named after a Yorkshireman but hailing from arid Mexico, he's a chameleon breed, of varied colouring and uncertain provenance.

Training notes

MAXIMUM SIZE: 20 cm (8 in) tall and 30 cm (1 ft) wide.

SOIL: Prefers his terrain gritty and porous; you might want to reward him with quarter-strength fertilizer during growing season, but don't do this more than once.

WATER: Demands a drink consistently in summer, but don't overindulge him: test that the soil's dry for an inch or two before you believe he's thirsty. In winter, water sparingly.

FLOWERS: All summer long; coral-yellow blooms dangle off arched stems up to 60 cm (2 ft) long.

WATCH OUT FOR: This guy's mean growth rate. He's a vigorous reproducer. Prune, or send his babies to new homes.

Styling notes

Fred's a shape-shifter of sundry complexions. In full sun, his leaves will reach full pink-purple potential, but you can put him in the shade too. He'll play it cool and turn teal blue.

Gymnocalycium mihanovichii

MOON CACTUS

Resembling a flashy shower cap, this perky plant mimics the moon, behaving like a little satellite: hopeless at making its own chlorophyll, it has to be grafted atop a friendly host. The result: a cactus with a planetary hairdo.

Training notes

MAXIMUM SIZE: 1.5 cm (½ in) across.

SOIL: Not fussy, just don't let the soil get soggy; a mix of sand and loam should keep this cactus content.

WATER: During the summer months, every week or so, for small plants especially. In winter, once in a blue moon.

FLOWERS: Aren't as standout as the cactus itself, but still dramatic: pink posers that spurt from the head.

WATCH OUT FOR: Relationship issues; after two years or so, your Moon Cactus is likely to grow apart from its partner – quite literally. You'll need to graft it to a new friend.

Styling notes

In its South American habitat, the Moon Cactus enjoys a home alternately shady and sunny, living among the bushes; don't let it blister in direct sunlight. A nice windowsill is perfect; or make it a sunny kitchen table centrepiece in a funky pot.

BOTTLE CACTUS

Don't bottle up your plant pet dreams! Let them out by indulging this quirky chum, whose dark green to purple bottle-shaped stems clump into an upright, bushy cluster.

Training notes

MAXIMUM SIZE: 60 cm (2 ft) tall.

SOIL: Hankers for rough soil (gritty and bitty); and, greedier than most, demands feeding with half-strength 10-10-10 balanced fertilizer every two weeks.

WATER: Little and often, to keep the soil moist but not soggy.

FLOWERS: A shower of little orange bells in late winter to early spring. Ding-dong!

WATCH OUT FOR: Plant fatigue! After flowering, needs a month-long rest with no feed and just a little water.

Styling notes

Bottle Cactus is also known as the Drunkard's Dream, which is perhaps why he's such a sleepyhead. Grumpy if he gets less than 14 hours' sleep, he'll appreciate you shutting out the light with a paper bag. Because this chap isn't generally a sun-lover, sit him in the middle of a bright room, perhaps in a hanging basket to let his bottles dangle.

ZEBRA CACTUS

You'll be surprised to hear that this striking set of stripes belongs to neither a zebra nor a cactus – it's actually a succulent! Originally hailing from South Africa, this spiky guy looks like the top of a pineapple, with long, dark-green leaves that taper to a point.

Training notes

MAXIMUM SIZE: A sluggish grower, this is a low-maintenance houseplant; 5 to 20 cm (2 to 8 in) is normal.

SOIL: A well-draining mix that includes some perlite, vermiculite, or coarse sand for drainage. Gets hungry monthly in growing season for a succulent feed.

WATER: Sparingly, except for in summer, when it'll want a monthly drink after its soil dries out.

FLOWERS: A mid-summer celebration of green-veined white blooms emerge on a thin stem up to 40 cm (16 in) tall.

WATCH OUT FOR: Too much sun – yellow or white leaves mean it's overdone it and needs to move to a shadier spot.

Styling notes

With its pointy green leaves and bumpy white stripes, the Zebra will happily feature in any plant collection. Make it a focal point – even go so far as to place it on a pedestal among darker-leaved companions.

ROLLING HEN AND CHICKS

Nurture this jewelled succulent and you'll end up adopting a whole family! Poultry by name, far from paltry in offspring, these verdant roses pop out baby plantlets very easily. New offshoots, attached only by precarious stems, often roll away from her to root.

Training notes

MAXIMUM SIZE: Leaves up to 4 cm (1½ in) wide, flower stems up to 20 cm (8 in) high.

SOIL: Roosts best in a slightly acidic soil, around pH 6.0. Satisfied by controlled-release fertilizer at start of summer.

WATER: In winter, once a month's plenty; gets thirstier throughout the growing season in summer and spring.

FLOWERS: The bulky, stalky efflorescence – either pale yellow or pink – is the mother hen's final statement before she dies. Happens anytime in summer.

WATCH OUT FOR: Root rot most foul. Don't overwater.

Styling notes

It's difficult to ruffle this hen's feathers. Able to withstand near-freezing temperatures, she is happy living on a cold windowsill with light shade to full sun.

Kalanchoe laetivirens

MOTHER OF THOUSANDS

Meet the Madagascan mothership of unusual greenery. A bizarre blue-green, she spawns her 'thousands' of babies at her leaves' edge, giving them a curious ruffled effect.

Training notes

MAXIMUM SIZE: Up to 60 cm (2 ft) tall.

SOIL: Ordinary potting soil mix suits this easygoing mummy, but she'll crave liquid fertilizer twice a week in the summer – you can also feed her slow-release pellets.

WATER: Cautiously in summertime, watching that the soil surface dries out first; she's not really thirsty in winter, but water if her fleshy leaves start to shrivel up.

FLOWERS: A coiffure of pale pink blooms in spring.

WATCH OUT FOR: Her leaves (poisonous!) and flowers (toxic). Don't just keep cats and dogs away; she's a defensive damsel and will give bare hands a nasty allergic reaction.

Styling notes

Fecund but fussy, the Mother of Thousands is a sun-seeker and has to be kept toasty warm (nothing below 12°C). Keep her somewhere bright; and if you're looking to accessorize, her blue-green cloaking would make a striking contrast with a maroon pot – experiment!

PANDA PLANT

Adorable oval leaves that are covered in fur and spotted with black (some say it looks like the ears of a cat!) will tempt you to 'pander' to this grey-green plant's every need. And some do, tickling its ears with a small dry paintbrush to keep it looking sharp.

Training notes

MAXIMUM SIZE: 1 m (3 ft) tall and 60 cm to 1 m (2 to 3 ft) wide.

SOIL: Enjoys a loam-based or sandy bed with good drainage; offer diluted fertilizer monthly from spring to autumn.

WATER: Hardly thirsty at all in winter, and even in summer, make sure the bed is dry before watering.

FLOWERS: Dinky, crimson, and bell-shaped, but generally too shy to peek out in captivity.

WATCH OUT FOR: Your pets might try to have a nibble of this furry favourite. Don't let them! It's toxic.

Styling notes

This velvet charmer is best trained in a room with a balance of brightness: some direct sunshine, some indirect, maybe some shade, if you can find a room to accommodate! As your Panda Plant grows, you can repot it in a hanging basket so it can stretch its stems.

Lithops salicola

STONE PLANT

With a name that means 'stony faced' in ancient Greek, you could be forgiven for thinking this guy, alien and tumescent, looks a bit weird and unfriendly. Really, it just craves love and grows always as a pair of leaves – a cute couple who spawn quickly!

Training notes

MAXIMUM SIZE: Never gets very tall – about 2.5 cm (1 in); after decades of growth might reach 25 cm (10 in) wide.

SOIL: Used to the rock crevices of southern Africa, so fond of sandy soil. But abstemious: no need to fertilize.

WATER: Fussier than most, it's dormant in summer and winter and might burst if you try to give it a drink during this time. Only thirsty when you notice it either blooming or growing (autumn and spring), but still, be careful.

FLOWERS: In autumn, daisy-like, up to 5 cm (2 in) across.

WATCH OUT FOR: Will scar if you overdo it on the liquid!

Styling notes

These living stones make an eclectic addition to a windowsill, or anywhere with bright, filtered light. Boast to your friends about how clever this fellow is: mimicking surrounding rocks and hiding most of its body under the soil, it only shows its leaf tips (fooling hungry herbivores).

PINCUSHION CACTUS

A bumpy Mexican marvel with a skin of spines, this is different from other cacti because, instead of ribs, it has tubercles: rounded protuberances for hoarding water.

Training notes

MAXIMUM SIZE: Grows outwards more than upwards, and can reach up to 45 cm (1½ ft) across. Each stem grows to 15 cm (6 in) tall.

SOIL: Lives happily in well-draining loam- and sand-based soil; gets a hankering for balanced liquid fertilizer every two to three weeks in summer.

WATER: Warily in winter, just enough to keep from shrivelling; more often from spring through to autumn but make sure the soil dries out between drinks.

FLOWERS: Small, often yellow-white, and buttercup-like; emerge in spring.

WATCH OUT FOR: Mealybugs and root rot.

Styling notes

This pincushion quickly becomes more of a pin-carpet if you indulge it with too much sun. Play with the spread by choosing different widths of pots – keep it tall in a narrow pot, or go for short and stubbly in a wider basin. Choose a bright room for this funky fellow.

BUNNY EARS CACTUS

No prizes for guessing how this buddy got its name. Ear-shaped green pads form the leporine outline of a plant who's cute but not cuddly. Studded with little prickles, Bunny Ears is best admired from a safe distance.

Training notes

MAXIMUM SIZE: 60 cm (2 ft) tall; stems up to 12 cm (5 in) wide.
SOIL: Perky in a sandy soil. Likes to be fed monthly in summer with low-nitrogen fertilizer, but stop one month before the beginning of winter.
WATER: In summertime, keep the soil moist but not sodden; in winter, though, impose a drought!
FLOWERS: Yellow to peachy; turn into little, purple-red fruits.
WATCH OUT FOR: Brown patches, either because of insect damage or a temperature drop.

Styling notes

This bunny likes it sunny for most of the year: keep it somewhere with strong light until late autumn, like a windowsill. But this rabbit has a habit of hibernating through winter and will need to be kept away from the central heating. Temperatures of 10 to 18°C are ideal. Will look adorable in any pot with its little ears sticking up.

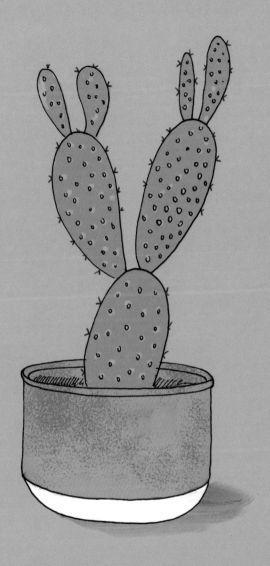

Opuntia vulgaris

EASTERN PRICKLY PEAR

A pear to beware: with thorny protrusions that are savagely sharp, it's easy to see why this green-pad plant is so warningly named. What's incredible is that it's also edible, producing fruit! The plant pads and juice have been used as a natural remedy, while the red fruit is often made into candy, and even wine.

Training notes

MAXIMUM SIZE: A huge 2 m (7 ft) tall; pads grow to 45 cm (18 in) wide.

SOIL: Loves a sandy, loamy bed; to tempt flowers, nourish with 5-10-10 fertilizer monthly from spring to autumn.

WATER: A desert cactus, it's not thirsty; once or twice a week in summer; in autumn and winter, once or twice a month.

FLOWERS: Knockout yellow; from spring onwards.

WATCH OUT FOR: Rot; act fast by amputating the mouldy parts and treating the cuts with insecticide.

Styling notes

Obviously, you're not going to want to sit your prickly pear somewhere it might injure you! A windowsill you can see but don't often go near might be best: it adores full sunlight, and the warm reminds it of its native Mexico.

OLD MAN OF THE ANDES

Cocooned in wispy white fur, this Old Man may look aged but he's far from frail. In the mountains of his native South America, his woolly coat protects him equally from light frost and searing sunlight.

Training notes

MAXIMUM SIZE: 60 cm (2 ft) tall – after 20 years.

SOIL: Enjoys a fair bit of grit in his well-drained compost (a ratio of one-third). Satiate with liquid fertilizer every one to two weeks in summer.

WATER: In summer, relatively often; let the soil surface dry out in between waterings. In winter, keep him dry.

FLOWERS: Tubes of bright red, but you'll only spot these once the cactus has reached a ripe old age, and even then, it's rare to spot in cultivated plants.

WATCH OUT FOR: Discolouration, which might happen if the room's dusty (simply brush him with warm soapy water to clean); very susceptible to root rot.

Styling notes

He enjoys an airy room with strong sunlight (to get through all that hair!). Give him a comb if he gets unkempt. He's a vigorous grower; repot him every 2 years.

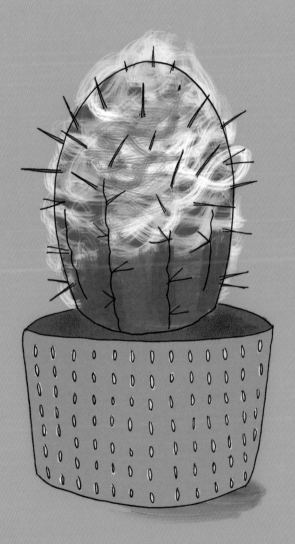

MEXICAN FENCE POST CACTUS

In Mexico, this columnar hunk, who grows upright but branches outwards at the base, is sturdy enough to function as a living fence along roadways, discouraging intruders with his spikes. He's extremely low maintenance as a houseplant and cute in a dinky pot.

Training notes

MAXIMUM SIZE: A massive 3.5 m (12 ft) tall in time.

SOIL: Puts up with potting soil; fertilizer unnecessary, though you can indulge him. His brother, *Pachycereus pringlei*, has developed the incredible ability to grow without soil, straight on rock!

WATER: Almost never. Remember: you want him to think he's still in the arid conditions of the Mexican desert.

FLOWERS: Pink to greenish, producing spiny yellow-red fruit.

WATCH OUT FOR: Overwatering (main cause of death).

Styling notes

Pachycereus is a seriously tough genus of cacti, producing some of the most towering specimens in the world. Difficult to offend, he would look good in a conservatory, or any room with lots of windows and plenty of sunlight.

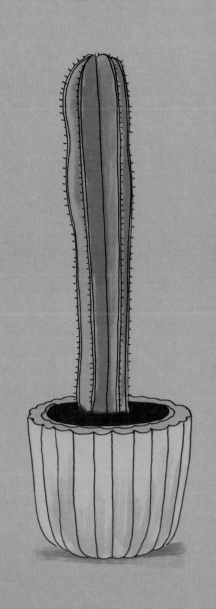

Pachyphytum oviferum

MOONSTONES

Moonstones is a beautifully resonant name for these luminescent plant eggs. In the rocky cliffs of Mexico, they grow in whorls of silver-green and are happy being neglected, making them a great choice for those lacking green fingers.

Training notes

MAXIMUM SIZE: Gradually forms dense clumps up to 25 cm (10 in) tall and about 30 cm (1 ft) wide.

SOIL: Tolerant of poor soil, but gratified by some gravel.

WATER: More in winter than summer, as it's active when it's colder. Prone to rotting so better to underdo its liquid diet: water only when you notice its leaves wilting.

FLOWERS: Scarlet, bell-shaped; winter to early spring.

WATCH OUT FOR: Mealybugs and excess moisture. If you get its soil a bit too wet, replace it entirely.

Styling notes

Moonstones, despite their delicate demeanour, are a hardy breed. Thriving in heat and in cold, in full or in partial light, they'll display even more vibrant colouring if you indulge their love of the sun. When looking to accessorize, try out a black pot and/or a layer of black pebbles on top of the soil to really set off the silvery hues.

108

Pilea peperomioides

CHINESE MONEY PLANT

Legend has it that if you plant a coin in the soil your Money Plant lives in, it will attract wealth. Sceptical? Well, this succulent's lovably odd button leaves will win you over regardless, waving at you like a tiny tree. It's not for nothing that this guy is one of the most sought-after houseplants and difficult to find in stock.

Training notes

MAXIMUM SIZE: 30 cm (12 in) spread, 30 cm (12 in) high.

SOIL: Cheerful if soil is sandy, chalky, and well-drained. Not too hungry for fertilizer; can feed monthly or so during its growth period (spring to early autumn), but not essential.

WATER: Best if you mist this moneypenny, rather than dousing with water. Active in the warmer months, it'll get thirstier then, but the soil should stay relatively dry.

FLOWERS: Pink, inconspicuous; may see them in summer.

WATCH OUT FOR: Root rot is a likely problem.

Styling notes

Will bring you the best return if you sit it in a bright room: it revels in indirect light. But this little chap's leaves have a tendency to search after the sun! Avoid this by turning the tables of fortune, as it were, rotating your plant weekly.

MOTHER-IN-LAW'S TONGUE

Her leaves are stiff, stylishly patterned in a marbled green, edged with gold, and razor sharp as this plant's namesake. But despite her bite, she has enjoyed a rich history of cultivation. Allow her to sanctify your home, flooding it with her promised eight virtues, as per Chinese tradition – or just let her jazz up your living room.

Training notes

MAXIMUM SIZE: Eventually 1 m (3 ft) tall (5 to 10 years).

SOIL: Only approves of alkaline or neutral sandy soil.

WATER: Err on the side of too little, especially in winter. Give a sporadic soaking, then discard excess water in the saucer.

FLOWERS: Alas, flowers just aren't really her style. If you're a rare witness, they're fragrant, greeny-white, and peek out from the top of her foliage.

WATCH OUT FOR: Vine weevils; root rot.

Styling notes

Sansevieria withers in the glare of too much sun: she'll protest by yellowing her leaves. Boldly architectural in form, she makes a statement centrepiece. She'll grow speedily provided she's kept warm (no lower than 10 to 15°C) and needs a new pot every year.

Schlumbergera x buckleyi

CHRISTMAS CACTUS

This festive friend flowers at Christmas and, in bloom, resembles a string of Christmas lights. Fleshy segmented stems with scalloped, leaf-like edges sub in for leaves and droop under their own weight. No spines in sight!

Training notes

MAXIMUM SIZE: 45 cm (18 in) wide and high.

SOIL: Comfy in cactus mix or loam-based soil; feed it liquid fertilizer during growing season (spring to autumn).

WATER: This jungle jingle-bell likes a bit more water and humidity than its desert counterparts. But let it rest during the winter, after its flowering season, and water just often enough that the soil doesn't completely dry out.

FLOWERS: Distinctive, brilliantly coloured trumpets can be up to three inches long. Famous, but may be difficult to coax out.

WATCH OUT FOR: Scorching; shrivelled stems (meaning it's too hot or sunny).

Styling notes

Find a semi-shady situation – well lit, but out of direct sun, with some humidity. A handy humidifying trick is to place the pot upon a gravel-filled saucer and keep the gravel moist. Pot-wise, think cosy Christmas jumper – your cactus won't grow well if its pot is too big.

Sedum morganianum

BURRO'S TAIL

Like a friendly, verdant Rapunzel, this adorable bushy succulent has trailing 'tails' composed of plump, juicy green droplet leaves – one of my favourites for its appearance and very easygoing nature.

Training notes

MAXIMUM SIZE: Branches can grow up to 60 cm (2 ft) long.

SOIL: Standard cactus mix works well; feed with a controlled-release fertilizer at the beginning of summer.

WATER: A thorough soak in spring and summer months, allowing the soil to become dry to the touch in between. Monthly is enough during winter; overwatering is the number one way to kill this plant, so err on the side of caution. You'll know you're underwatering if it develops dry, brown leaf spots.

FLOWERS: A late summer event; hanging clusters of small red, yellow or white blossoms.

WATCH OUT FOR: Wilting or soft leaves (this means you're overwatering); root rot; delicate leaves (handle gently!).

Styling notes

Burro is a dainty choice for hanging baskets or perches. Likes sun but can burn in hot, full sunlight – a windowsill or shelf spot is ideal.

JELLY BEAN PLANT

Short, jelly bean-shaped drops cling to sprawling, leaning stems. These yellowy-green leaves are tipped in reddish brown and can bronze in the summer sun, leading to the alternative nickname of 'Pork and Beans Plant'.

Training notes

MAXIMUM SIZE: About 30 cm (1 ft) tall.

SOIL: Anything well-draining; succulent or cactus mix works well. Fertilize monthly in spring and summer with a cactus/succulent fertilizer.

WATER: More regularly in spring/summer but let it dry out in between. Used to drought, so better to underwater.

FLOWERS: Bright yellow star-shaped blooms emerge from in between the leaves in mid-spring.

WATCH OUT FOR: Its toxicity – ironic given its delectable nicknames. This Bean is poisonous to people and pets.

Styling notes

The jelly bean likes full sun with some direct sunlight; does best on hot balconies or windowsills. Will accept normal humidity but appreciates some air circulation in summer. A squat pot or hanging basket with wispy trailing plants to accompany looks really cute, or have it hang out under a taller plant to add texture to a plant party.

Sempervivum arachnoideum

COBWEB HOUSELEEK

Ancient vegetable from the back of your fridge or cute fuzzy leaf saucer? The latter is a member of the *Sempervivum* genus and looks like the result of an artsy spider weaving inside a cabbage. With its mat-forming growth pattern, you might find these cobwebs spreading.

Training notes

MAXIMUM SIZE: 10 cm (4 in) high; 10 to 45 cm (4 in to 1½ ft) wide – over 5 to 10 years.

SOIL: Well-draining soil, with some added grit. Boost with slow-release fertilizer once a year when repotting.

WATER: Regularly in summer, ensuring soil dries between drinks; go easy in the winter: things can easily turn rotten.

FLOWERS: Star-shaped pink or pale yellow dainties shoot up from long stalks up to 12 cm (5 in) tall!

WATCH OUT FOR: Vine weevils; rust (a fungal disease indicated by yellow/brown/black/white pustules on leaves), which usually appears in mid-to-late summer or autumn.

Styling notes

With its protective coat, there's no fear of scorching this Cobweb, so full sunlight is the way to go. Low bowls are pretty – pair with smooth succulents like Echeveria or Aeonium for contrast.

Senecio mandraliscae

BLUE CHALK STICKS

A cool character that grows in a mat pattern, forming a silvery-blue bed of upward-reaching leaves. These ghostly fingers are textured like a plum's skin, with a whitish, chalky bloom on their surface.

Training notes

MAXIMUM SIZE: 30 to 45 cm (12 to 18 in) long, 60 cm to 1 m (24 to 36 in) wide.

SOIL: Sandy and well-draining; give it a light annual fertilizer dose, but don't overindulge it or it will grow too fast and flop over under its own weight!

WATER: Nonchalantly – will not notice if several weeks pass without it. Water most often in spring, sparingly in summer/autumn and not at all over the winter. Ensure that all water drains off before giving it a drink.

FLOWERS: Tiny and white and appear in summer.

WATCH OUT FOR: Overwatering; enthusiastic growth (you can repot and/or administer a trim when leaves flop; best to do this pruning in late summer).

Styling notes

Little ones like to be kept warm; light afternoon shade is nice somewhere airy and dry, like a hanging basket in a living room. This blue character will much enjoy a summer field trip outside.

PLANT FINDER

BUYER'S GUIDE

Cacti and succulents can be found just about anywhere: flower shops, markets, garden centres, hardware and home stores and even plant boutiques! Charity shops, discount stores and antique shops are all great sources for pots and vessels – especially non-traditional pieces that can be repurposed as planters!

Here is a list of shops and resources. All have online shops and many can ship plants across the country. In the UK try looking for your local British Cactus and Succulent Society.

UK

CONSERVATORY ARCHIVES
493-495 Hackney Road
London, E2 9ED
conservatoryarchives.co.uk

NEW COVENT GARDEN MARKET
London, SW8 5BH
newcoventgardenmarket.com/flowers

PRICK
492 Kingsland Rd,
London E8 4AE
prickldn.com

BOTANIQUE
London, locations in
Exmouth Market, Stoke
Newington and Brixton.
botaniqueworkshop.com

SQUIRE'S GARDEN CENTRES
Various locations in
South-East England
squiresgardencentres.co.uk

SURREAL SUCCULENTS
Tremenheere Sculpture
Gardens, Gulval, TR20 8YL
surrealsucculents.co.uk

WILKO
Various locations across UK
wilko.com

NARCISSUS FLOWERS AND PLANTS
87 Broughton Street
Edinburgh EH1 3RJ
narcissusflowers.co.uk

PUGHS GARDEN VILLAGE
Tynant Nurseries
Morganstown, Radyr
Cardiff CF15 8LB
pughsgardencentre.co.uk

SUCCULENTS WALES
Online-only
succulentswales.co.uk

BEST BUDS BELFAST
Black Staff Mill, 81–129
Springfield Road
Belfast BT127AB,
Northern Ireland
www.bestbudsbelfast.co.uk

URBAN PLANT LIFE
110–111 Cork Street,
Dublin 8,
Republic of Ireland
www.plantlife.ie

AUSTRALIA

BUNNINGS WAREHOUSE
Various locations across
NZ, Australia and UK
bunnings.co.au

FICKLE PRICKLES
Online-only, ships across
Western Australia
fickleprickles.com.au

AUSTRALIAN DESERT BLOOMS
Ipswich QLD 4300
cactiandsucculentsrus.com.au

NEW ZEALAND

BUNNINGS WAREHOUSE
bunnings.co.nz

PALMERS
Various locations,
North Island
palmers.co.nz

WAIRERE NURSERY
Waitakere, Auckland
succulents.co.nz